THE SECRET SOCIETY OF MONSTER HUNTERS

The Poltergeist's Haunting

by Kate Tremaine

illustrated by Jared Sams

Torch Graphic Press

Published in the United States of America by Cherry Lake Publishing Group
Ann Arbor, Michigan
www.cherrylakepublishing.com

Reading Adviser: Marla Conn, MS, Ed., Literacy specialist, Read-Ability, Inc.

Book Design: Book Buddy Media

Photo Credits: page 1: ©nazarkru/iStock / Getty Images; page 9: ©Michael Ochs Archives / Getty Images; page 11: ©Jan Engel / Shutterstock; page 11: ©OpenClipart-Vectors / Pixabay; page 13: ©Fiamma Corona / Shutterstock; page 27: ©DigitalVision Vectors/RobinOlimb / Getty Images; background: ©cienpies/iStock / Getty Images; background: ©OpenClipart-Vectors / Pixabay (facts); background: ©MarjanNo / Pixabay (lined paper); background: ©Nadiia Kalameiets / Shutterstock (sidebars)

Torch Graphic Press is an imprint of Cherry Lake Publishing Group.

Library of Congress Cataloging-in-Publication Data
Names: Tremaine, Kate, author. | Sams, Jared, illustrator.
Title: The poltergeist's haunting / by Kate Tremaine ; illustrated by Jared Sams.
Description: Ann Arbor, Michigan : Torch Graphic Press, 2020. | Series: The Secret Society of Monster Hunters | Includes bibliographical references and index. | Audience: Ages 10-13. | Audience: Grades 4-6. | Summary: Amy, Elena, and Jorge travel to Seattle in 1996 to find a rampaging poltergeist.
Identifiers: LCCN 2020017208 (print) | LCCN 2020017209 (ebook) | ISBN 9781534169456 (hardcover) | ISBN 9781534171138 (paperback) | ISBN 9781534172975 (pdf) | ISBN 9781534174818 (ebook)
Subjects: LCSH: Graphic novels. | CYAC: Graphic novels. | Poltergeists—Fiction. | Time travel—Fiction. | Secret societies—Fiction. | Seattle (Wash.)—History—20th century—Fiction.
Classification: LCC PZ7.7.T7 Po 2020 (print) | LCC PZ7.7.T7 (ebook) | DDC 741.5/973—dc23
LC record available at https://lccn.loc.gov/2020017208
LC ebook record available at https://lccn.loc.gov/2020017209

Cherry Lake Publishing Group would like to acknowledge the work of the Partnership for 21st Century Learning, a Network of Battelle for Kids. Please visit http://www.battelleforkids.org/networks/p21 for more information.

Printed in the United States of America
Corporate Graphics

TABLE OF CONTENTS

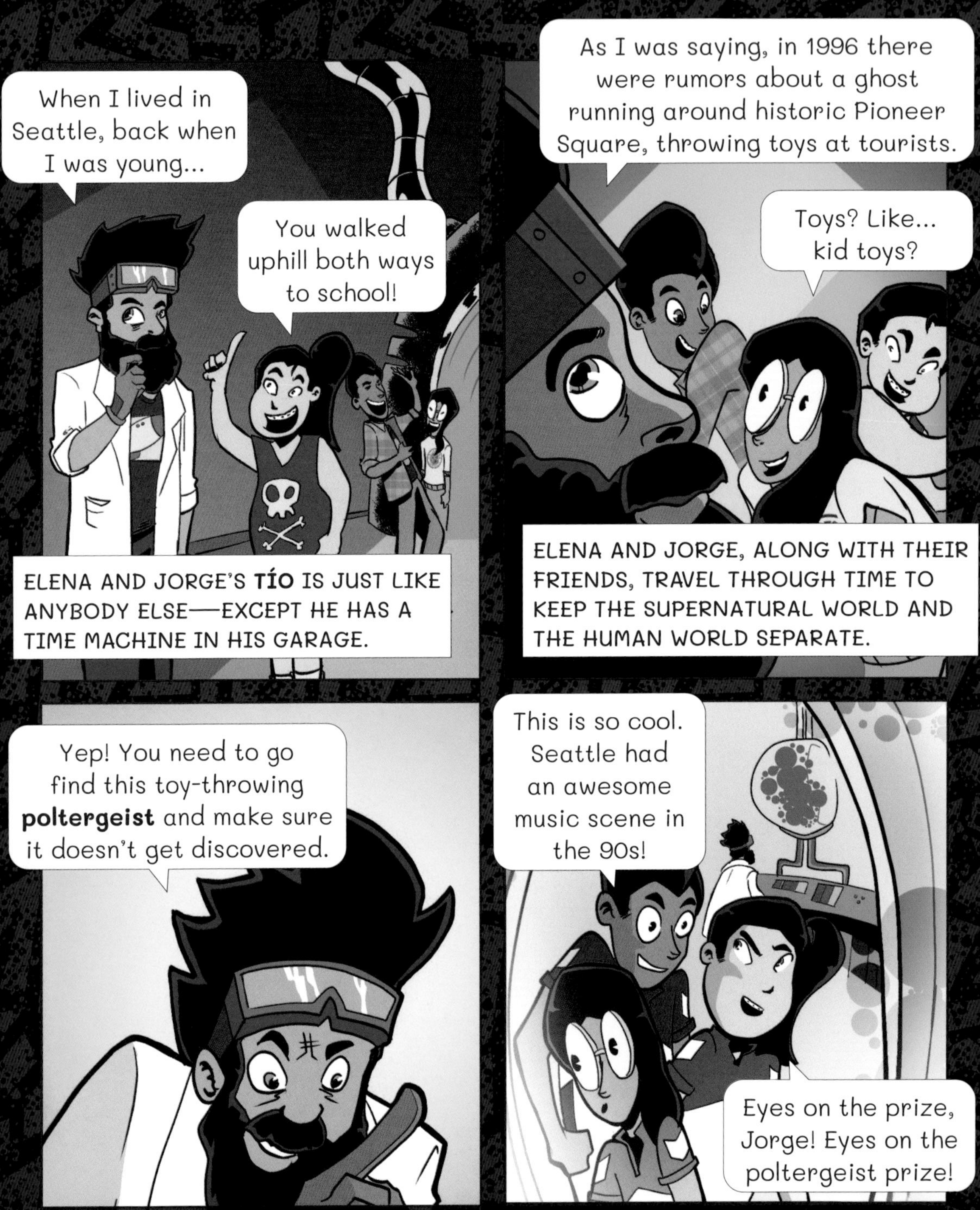
When I lived in Seattle, back when I was young...
You walked uphill both ways to school!
ELENA AND JORGE'S **TÍO** IS JUST LIKE ANYBODY ELSE—EXCEPT HE HAS A TIME MACHINE IN HIS GARAGE.
As I was saying, in 1996 there were rumors about a ghost running around historic Pioneer Square, throwing toys at tourists.
Toys? Like... kid toys?
ELENA AND JORGE, ALONG WITH THEIR FRIENDS, TRAVEL THROUGH TIME TO KEEP THE SUPERNATURAL WORLD AND THE HUMAN WORLD SEPARATE.
Yep! You need to go find this toy-throwing **poltergeist** and make sure it doesn't get discovered.
This is so cool. Seattle had an awesome music scene in the 90s!
Eyes on the prize, Jorge! Eyes on the poltergeist prize!

tío: "uncle" in Spanish

poltergeist: a ghost or supernatural being that causes loud noises, flying objects, and other physical disturbances

TIPS FOR THE DECADE

The Cold War ended in 1991 when the Soviet Union fell. Bill Clinton was president for most of the 1990s. To many Americans, it felt like a hopeful time. But to other Americans, things weren't so simple.

* Same-sex marriage was illegal.
* The country was starting to become aware of continued racism against African Americans.
* **Domestic terrorism** also began to increase during this decade.

Pop culture became huge in the 90s.

* Grunge, a kind of rock music, started in Seattle, Washington.
* Rhythm & blues (R&B) singers like Mariah Carey and Whitney Houston became megastars.
* Pop stars like the Spice Girls and Britney Spears became popular near the end of the decade.
* Hip-hop became more mainstream. Groups like the Fugees and De La Soul and stars like 2Pac and Snoop Dogg helped define the decade.

DE LA SOUL

domestic terrorism: terrorist acts where victims within the offender's own country are targeted

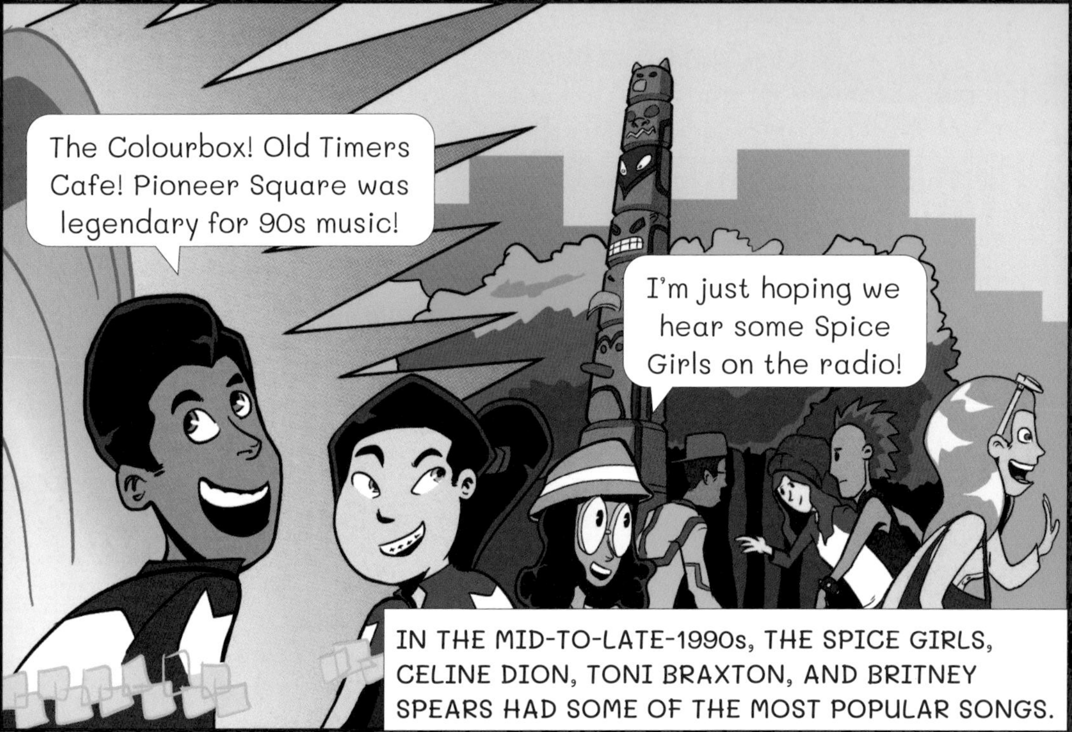
The Colourbox! Old Timers Cafe! Pioneer Square was legendary for 90s music!
I'm just hoping we hear some Spice Girls on the radio!
IN THE MID-TO-LATE-1990s, THE SPICE GIRLS, CELINE DION, TONI BRAXTON, AND BRITNEY SPEARS HAD SOME OF THE MOST POPULAR SONGS.

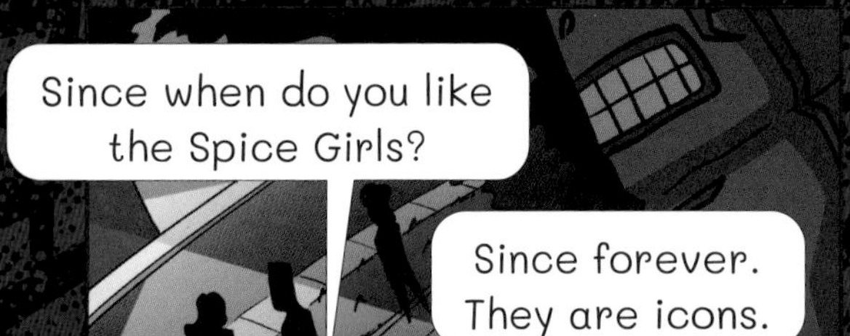
Since when do you like the Spice Girls?
Since forever. They are icons.
The Spice Girls were a British girl group. They became the best-selling girl group of all time. Their hit single "Wannabe" came out in 1996.

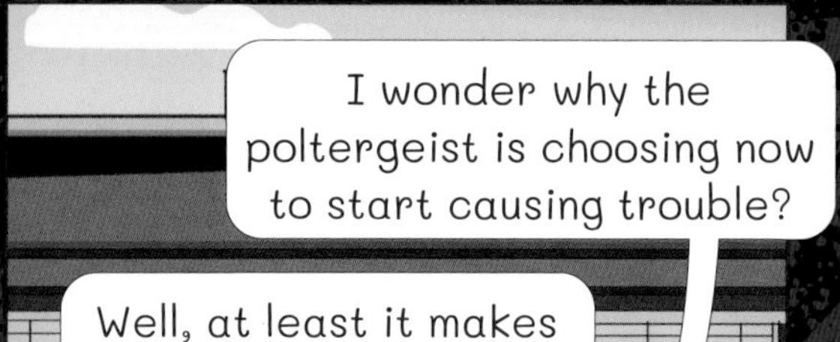
I wonder why the poltergeist is choosing now to start causing trouble?
Well, at least it makes sense that it's *here*, in the most historic district of Seattle.
PIONEER SQUARE WAS WHERE THE FOUNDERS OF SEATTLE SETTLED IN 1852. IT WAS THE CENTER OF THE CITY FOR A LONG TIME.

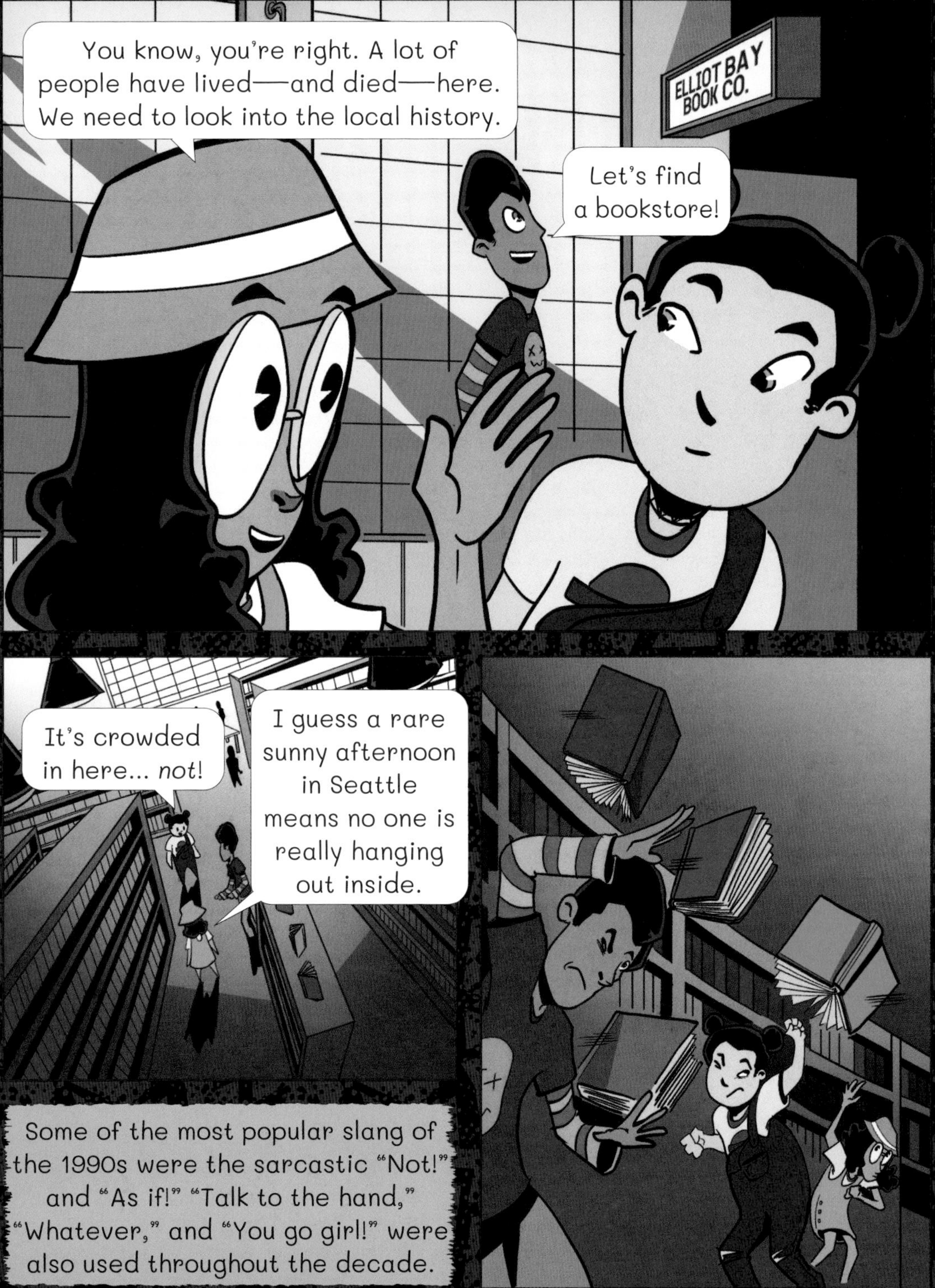
You know, you're right. A lot of people have lived—and died—here. We need to look into the local history.
ELLIOT BAY BOOK CO.
Let's find a bookstore!
It's crowded in here... *not*!
I guess a rare sunny afternoon in Seattle means no one is really hanging out inside.
Some of the most popular slang of the 1990s were the sarcastic "Not!" and "As if!" "Talk to the hand," "Whatever," and "You go girl!" were also used throughout the decade.

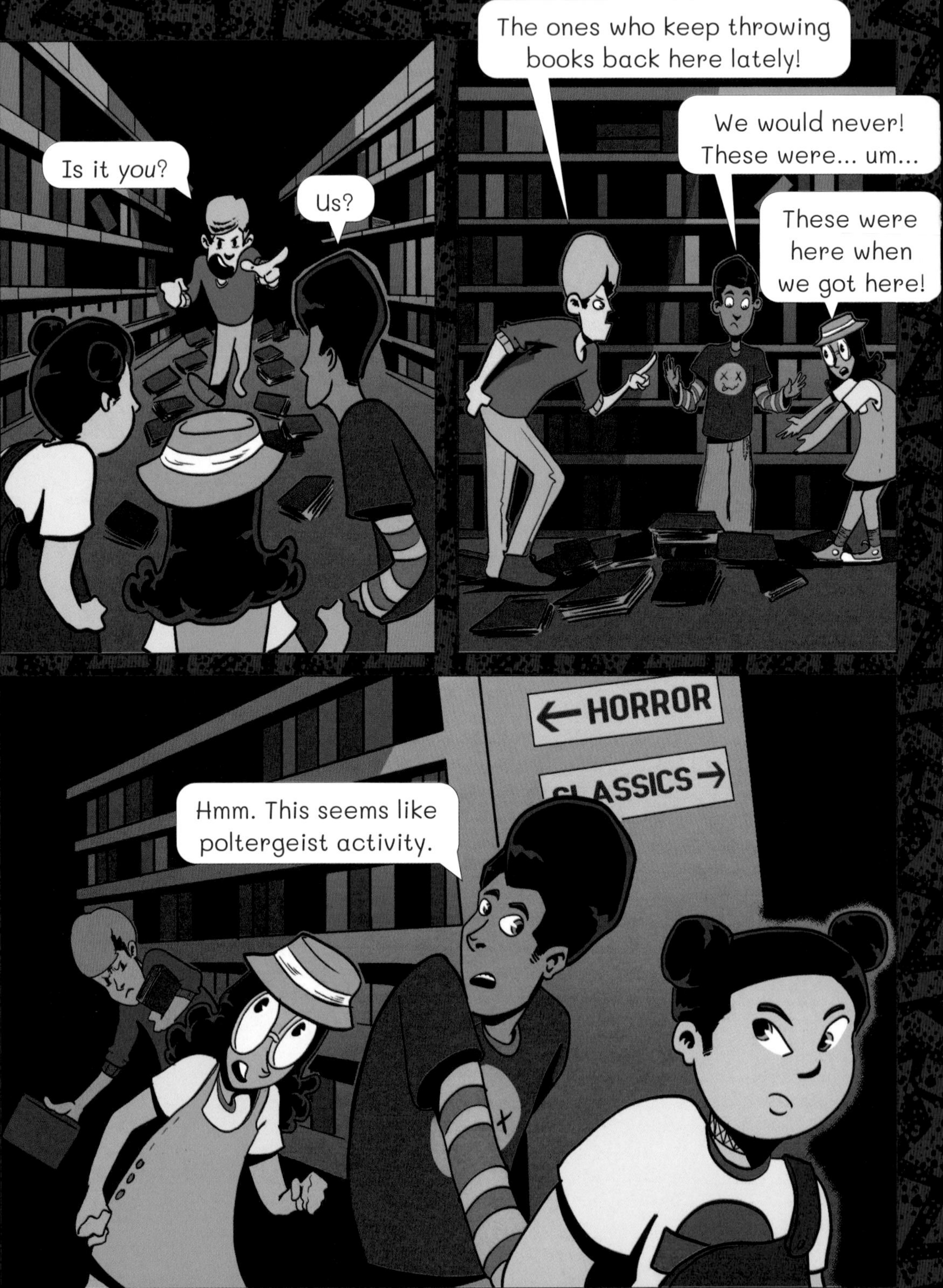

Is it *you*?
Us?
The ones who keep throwing books back here lately!
We would never! These were... um...
These were here when we got here!
←HORROR
CLASSICS→
Hmm. This seems like poltergeist activity.

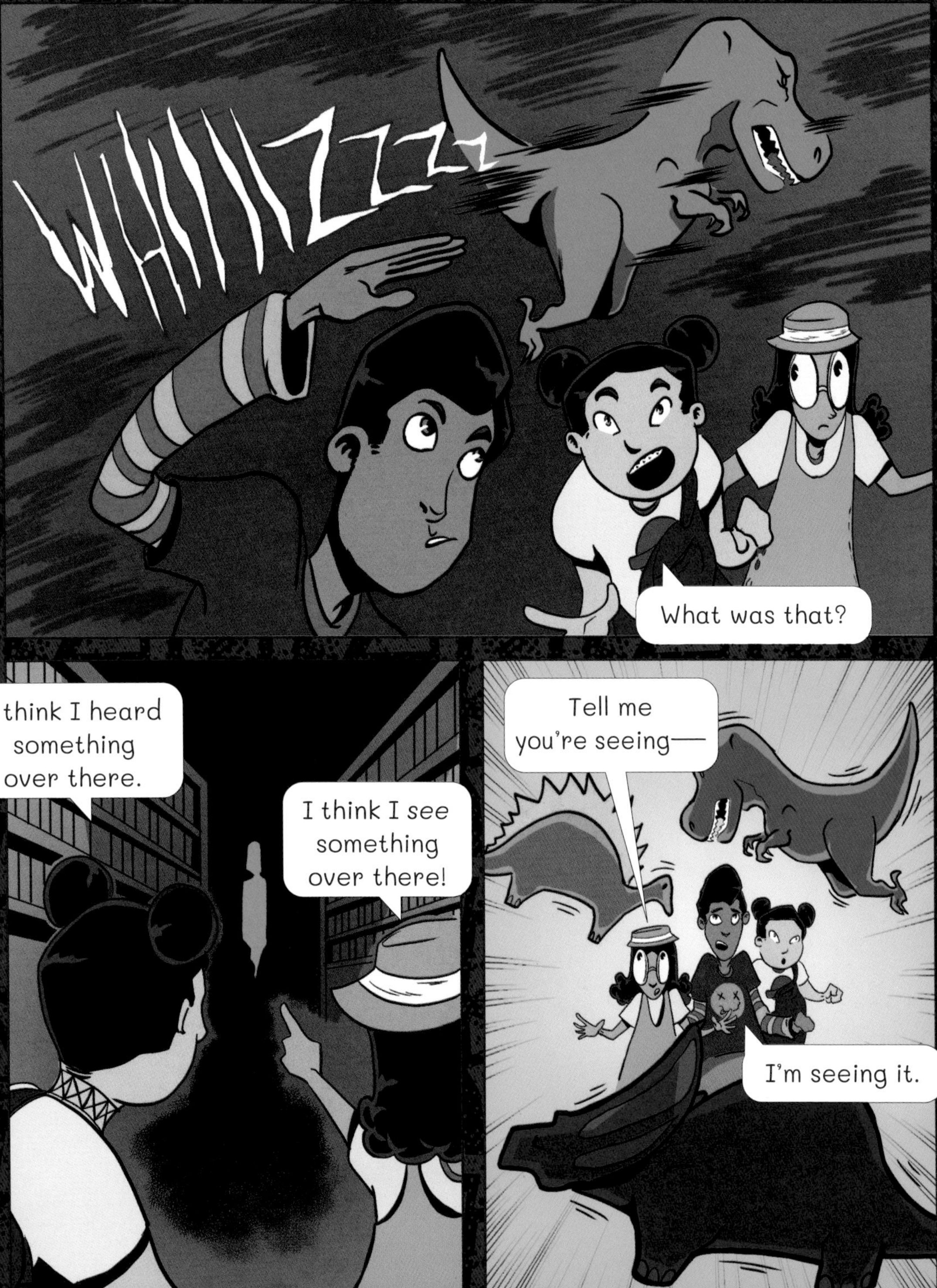
WHIIIIZzzzz
What was that?
I think I heard something over there.
I think I *see* something over there!
Tell me you're seeing—
I'm seeing it.

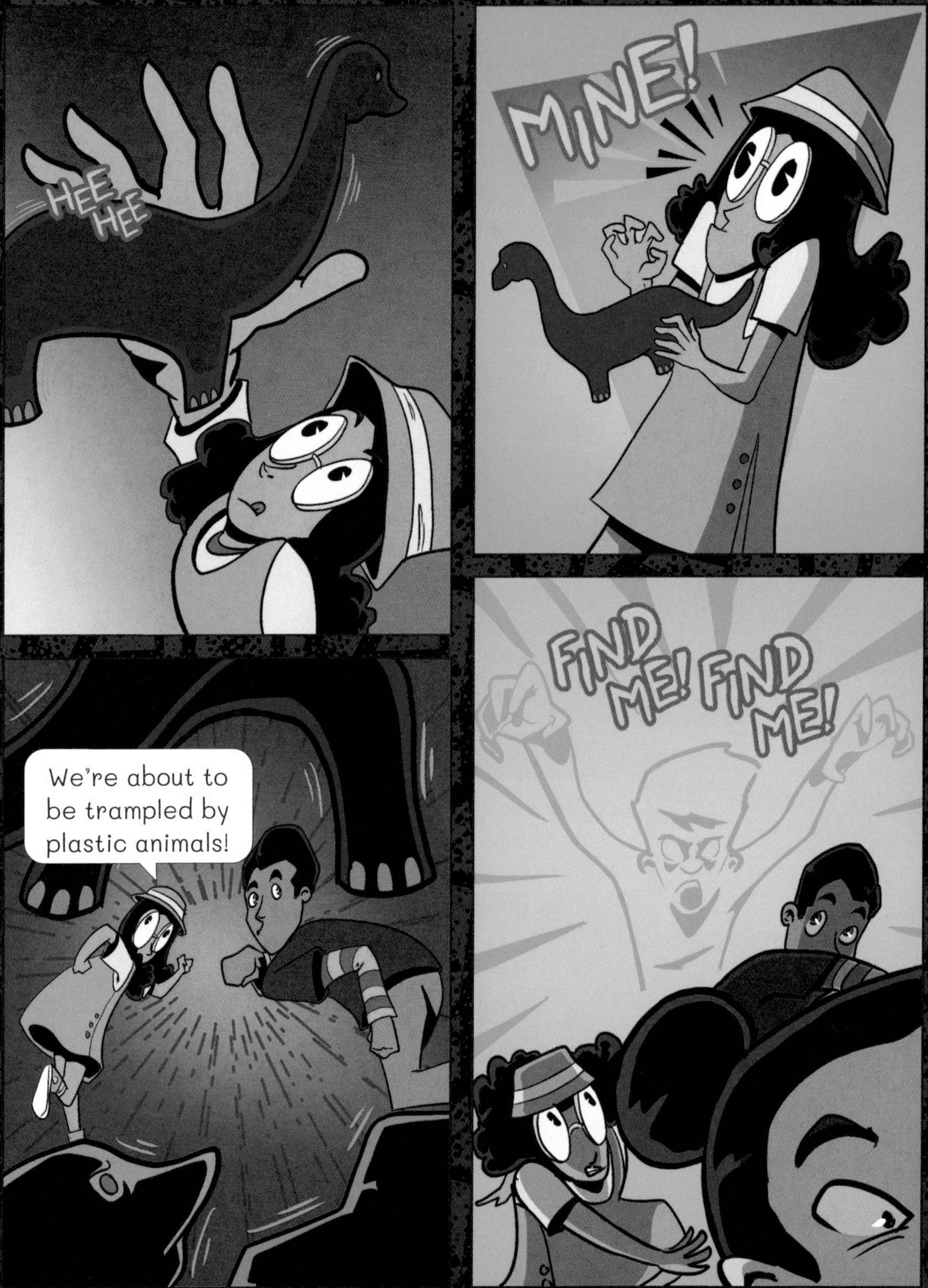
HEE HEE
MINE!
We're about to be trampled by plastic animals!
FIND ME! FIND ME!

PACKING LIST

In the 90s, grunge fashion was one popular style.

* It originated in Seattle.

* Both young men and women wore dark, baggy flannel shirts over torn jeans.

* Many people wore combat-style boots from English brand Doc Marten.

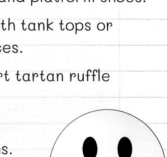

Grunge wasn't the only style.

* Many teen girls wore ringer tees, wide-leg jeans, chokers, barrettes, and platform shoes.

* Overalls or carpenter jeans worn with tank tops or thrift-store tees were popular choices.

* Short empire waist dresses and short tartan ruffle skirts were worn for a preppy style.

* Other fashions included smiley-face tees, tube tops, and hip-hugger jeans.

* Boys wore baggy button-down shirts in bold prints, and baggy jeans or khakis.

* Skater shoes were popular.

Hip-hop fashion was growing in popularity.

* At the time, this included sideways baseball caps.

* Baggy tracksuits and bomber jackets were also popular.

* Gold chains and Timberland boots completed the look.

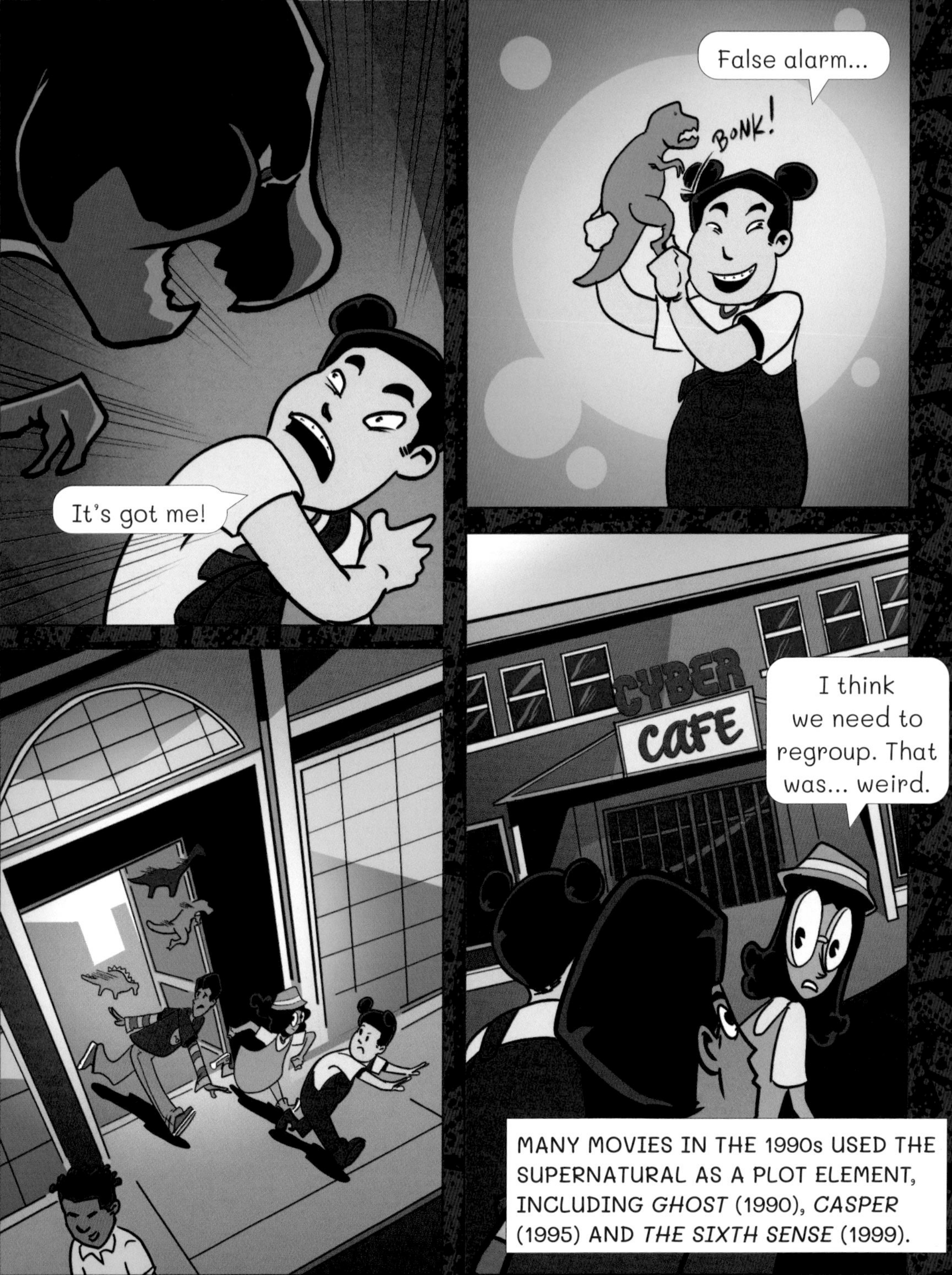
It's got me!
False alarm...
BONK!
CYBER
CAFE
I think we need to regroup. That was... weird.
MANY MOVIES IN THE 1990s USED THE SUPERNATURAL AS A PLOT ELEMENT, INCLUDING *GHOST* (1990), *CASPER* (1995) AND *THE SIXTH SENSE* (1999).

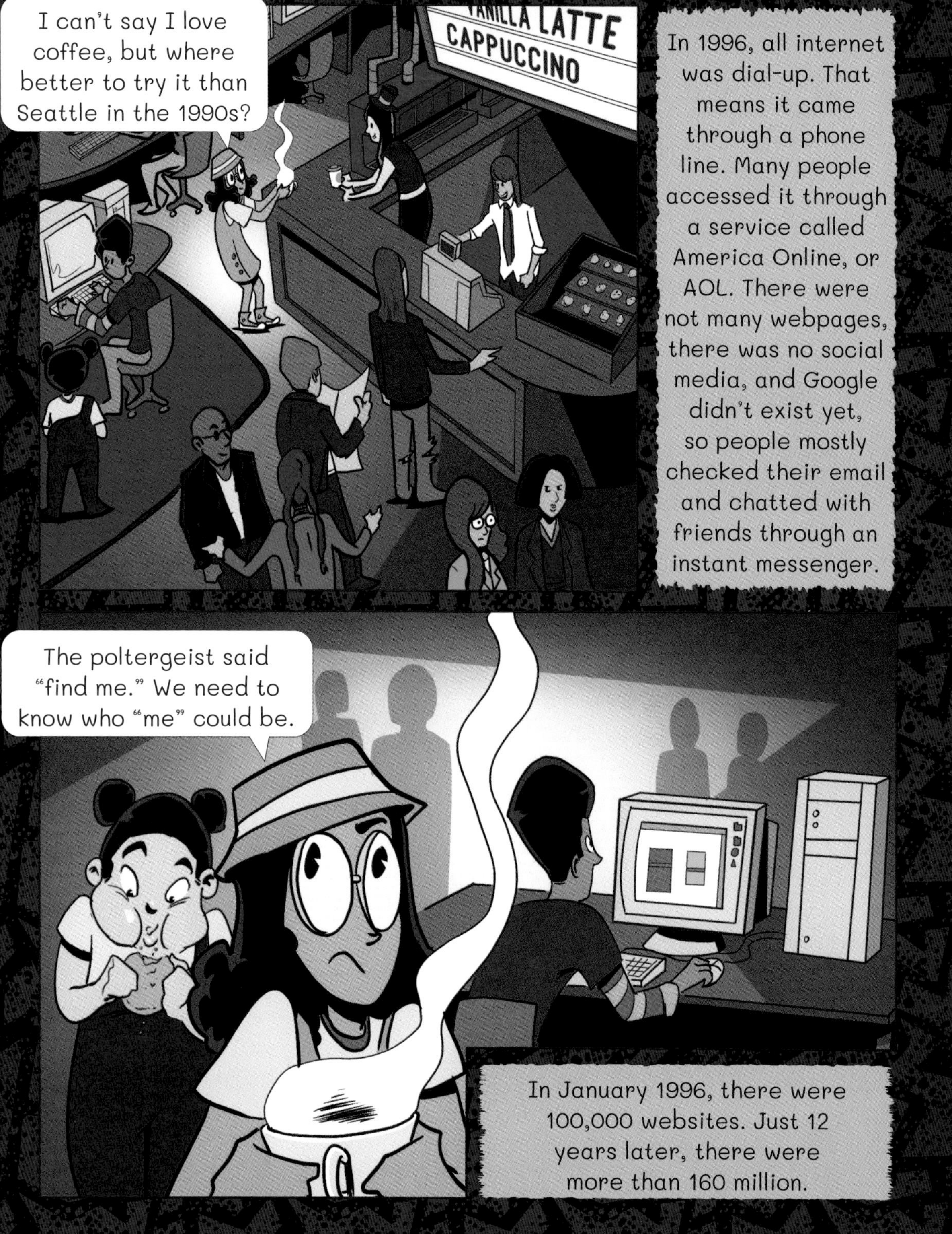
I can't say I love coffee, but where better to try it than Seattle in the 1990s?
VANILLA LATTE
CAPPUCCINO
In 1996, all internet was dial-up. That means it came through a phone line. Many people accessed it through a service called America Online, or AOL. There were not many webpages, there was no social media, and Google didn't exist yet, so people mostly checked their email and chatted with friends through an instant messenger.
The poltergeist said "find me." We need to know who "me" could be.
In January 1996, there were 100,000 websites. Just 12 years later, there were more than 160 million.

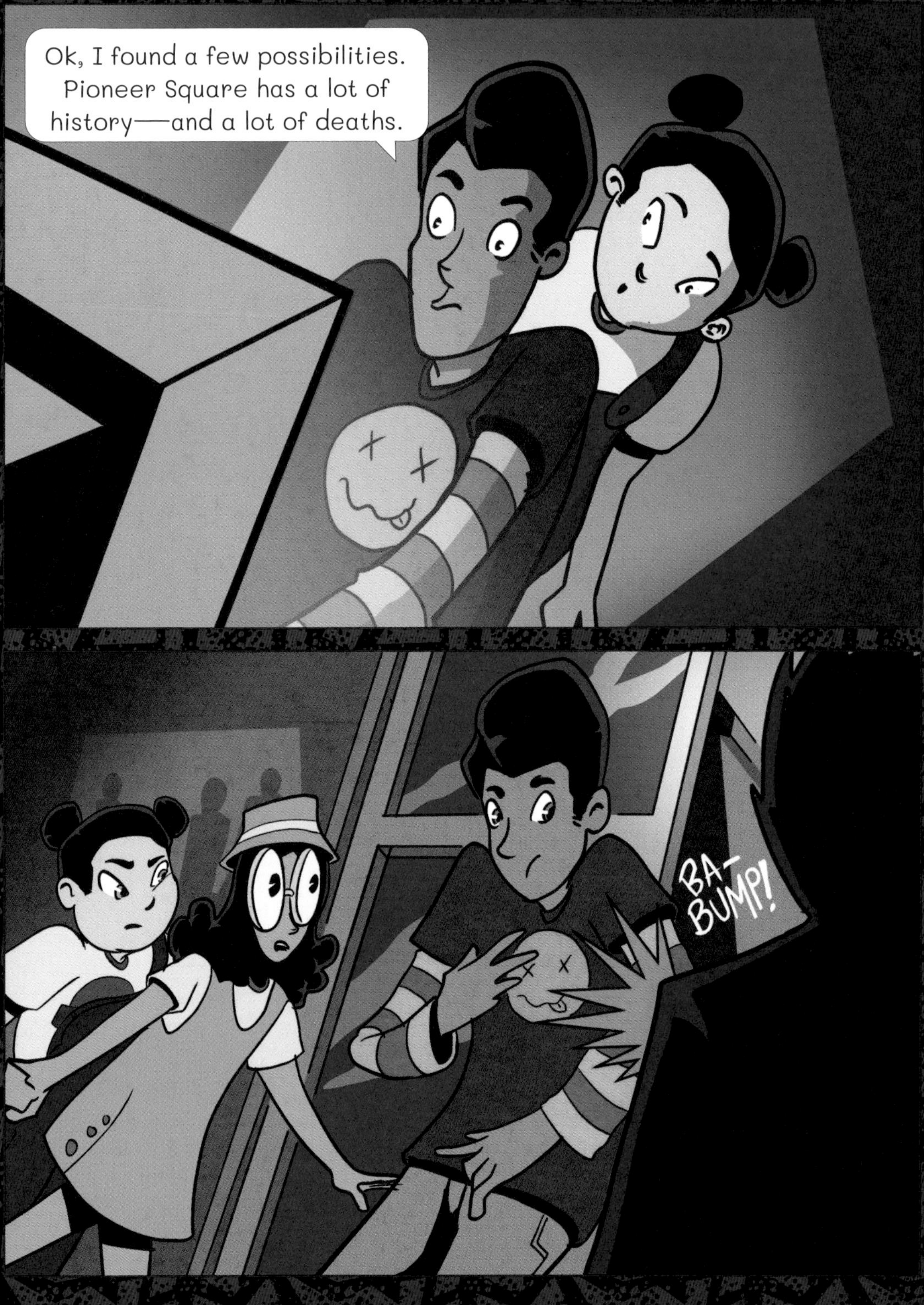
Ok, I found a few possibilities. Pioneer Square has a lot of history—and a lot of deaths.
BA-BUMP!

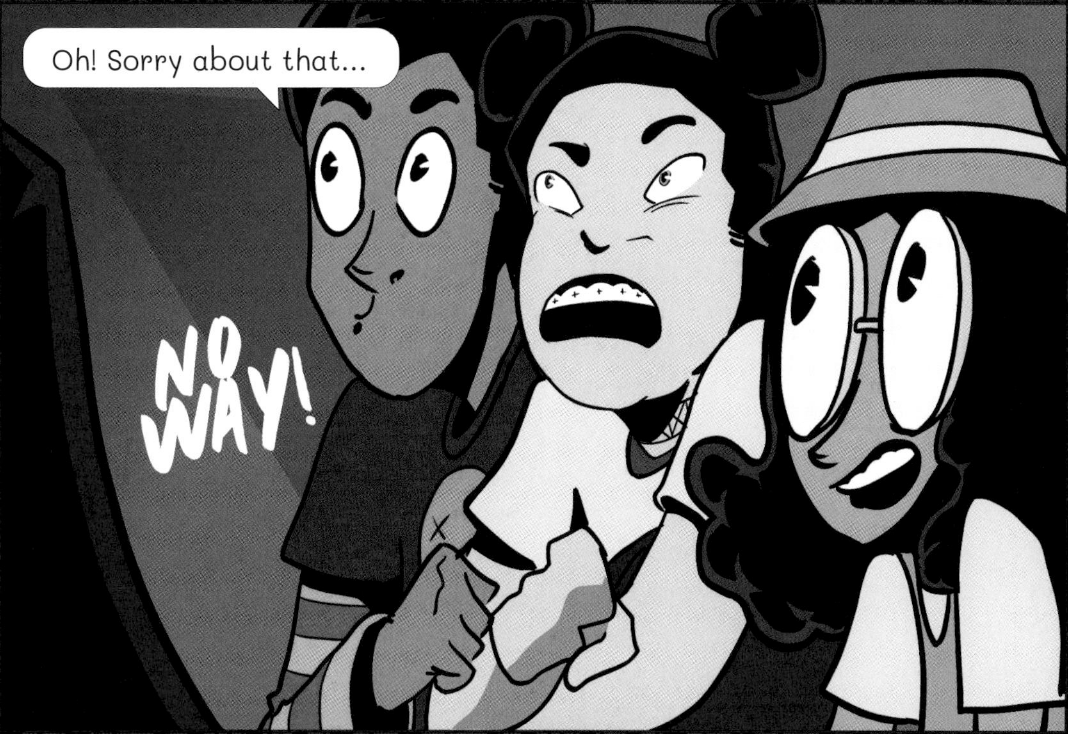
Oh! Sorry about that...
NO WAY!

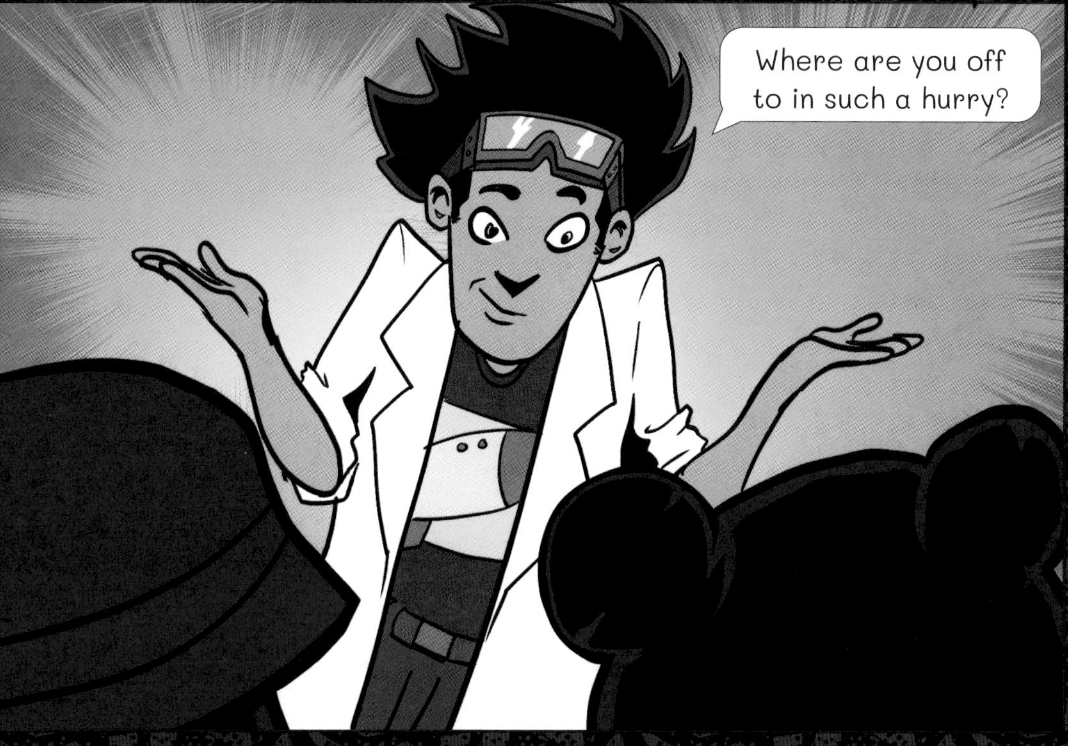
Where are you off to in such a hurry?

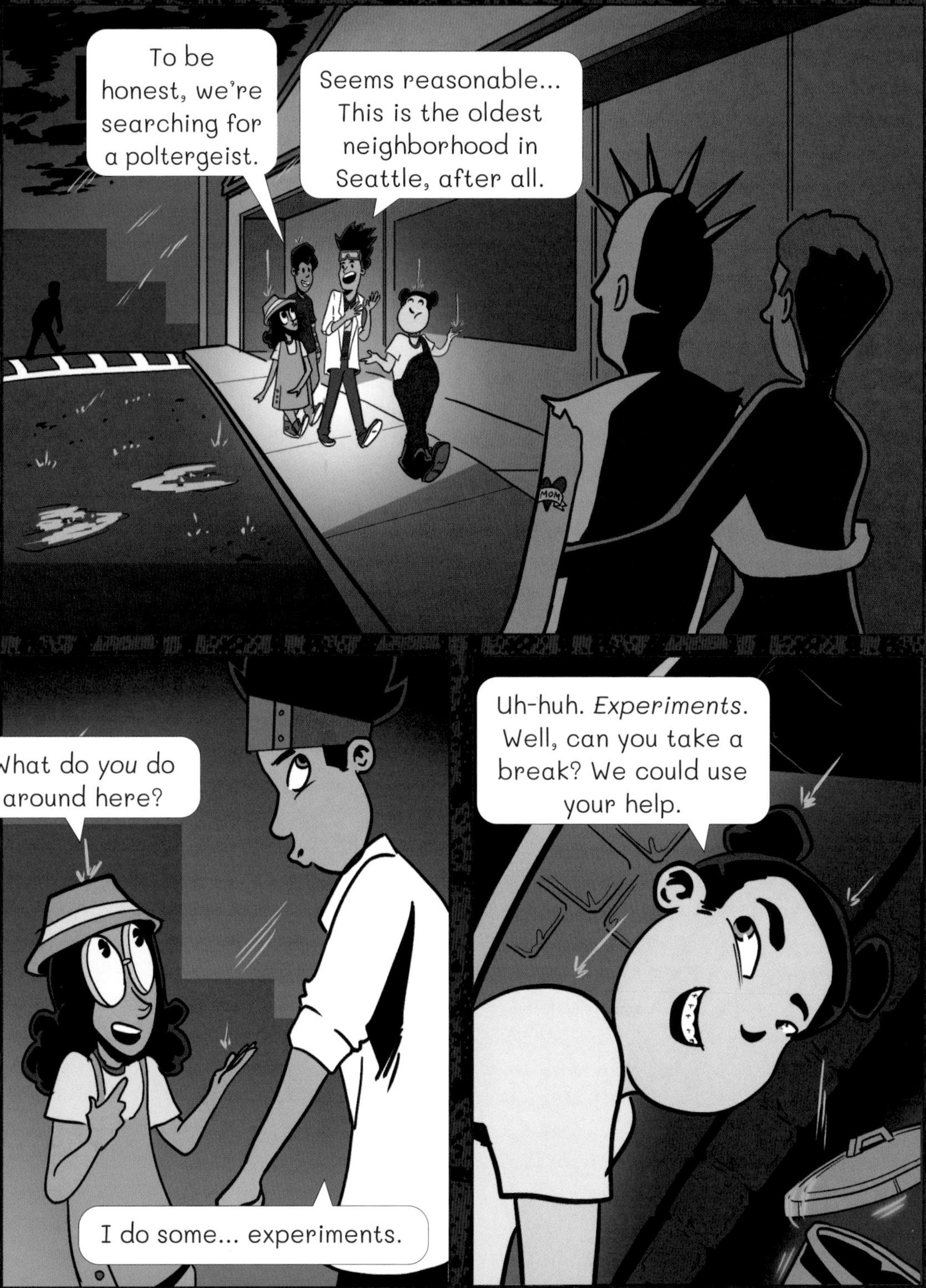
To be honest, we're searching for a poltergeist.
Seems reasonable... This is the oldest neighborhood in Seattle, after all.
MOM
What do *you* do around here?
I do some... experiments.
Uh-huh. *Experiments*. Well, can you take a break? We could use your help.

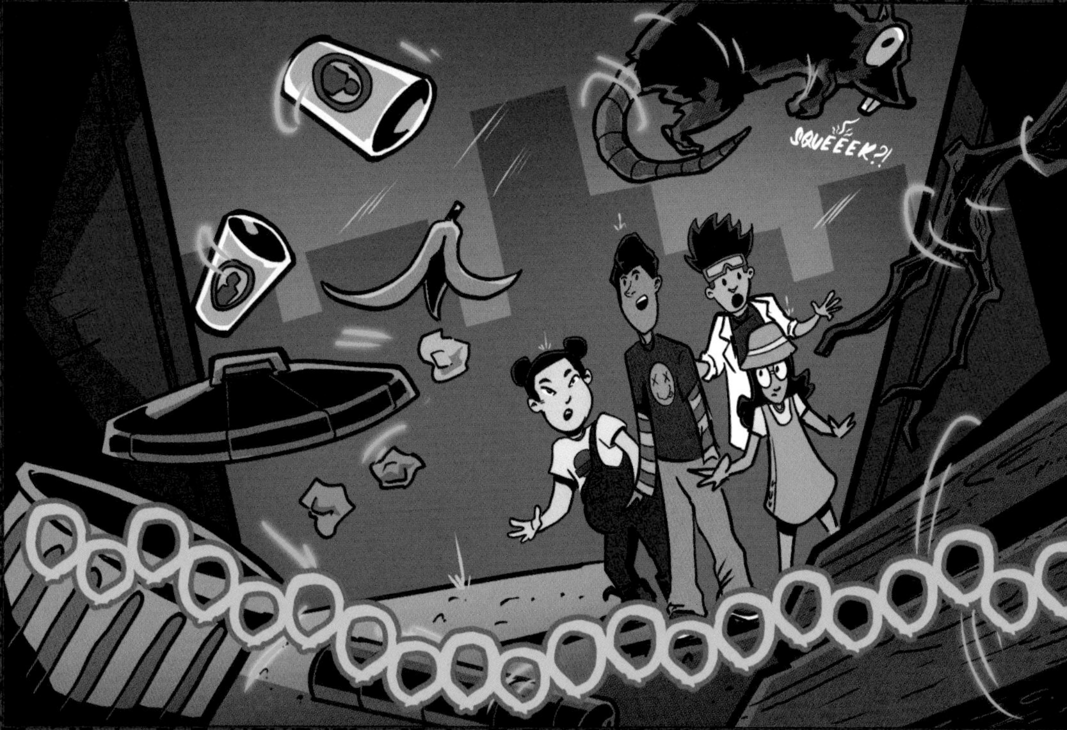
SQUEEEK?!
OOOOOOOOOOOOOOOOOOOOOOOOOO

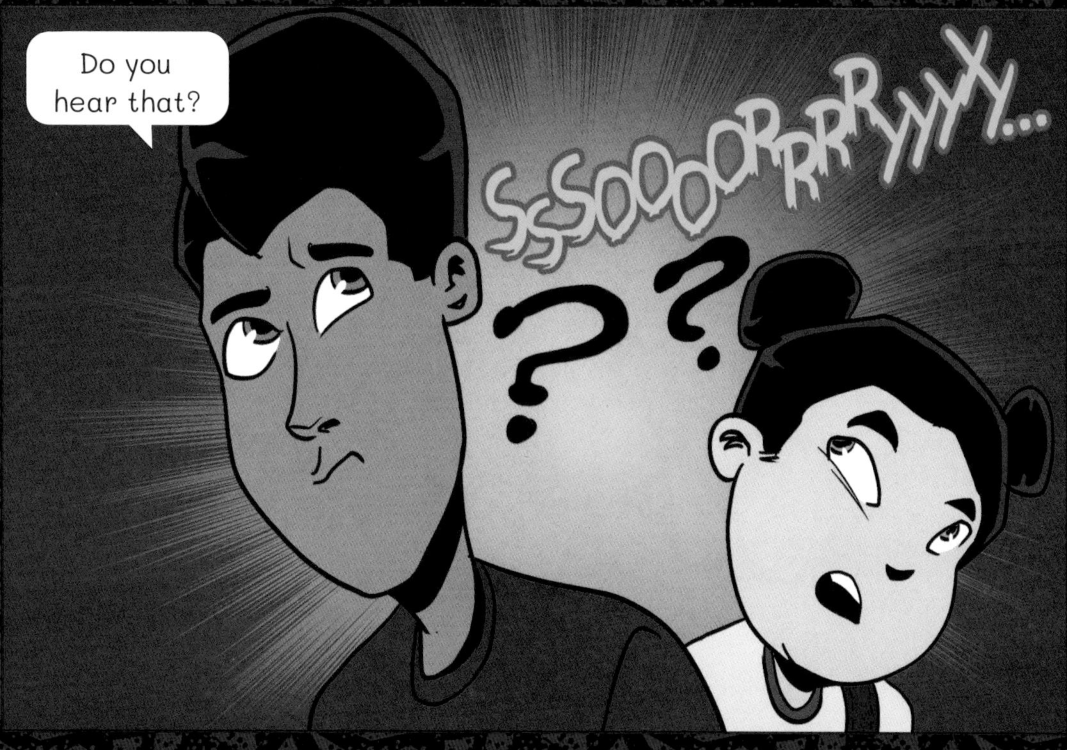
Do you hear that?
SSSOOOORRRRYYYY...
??

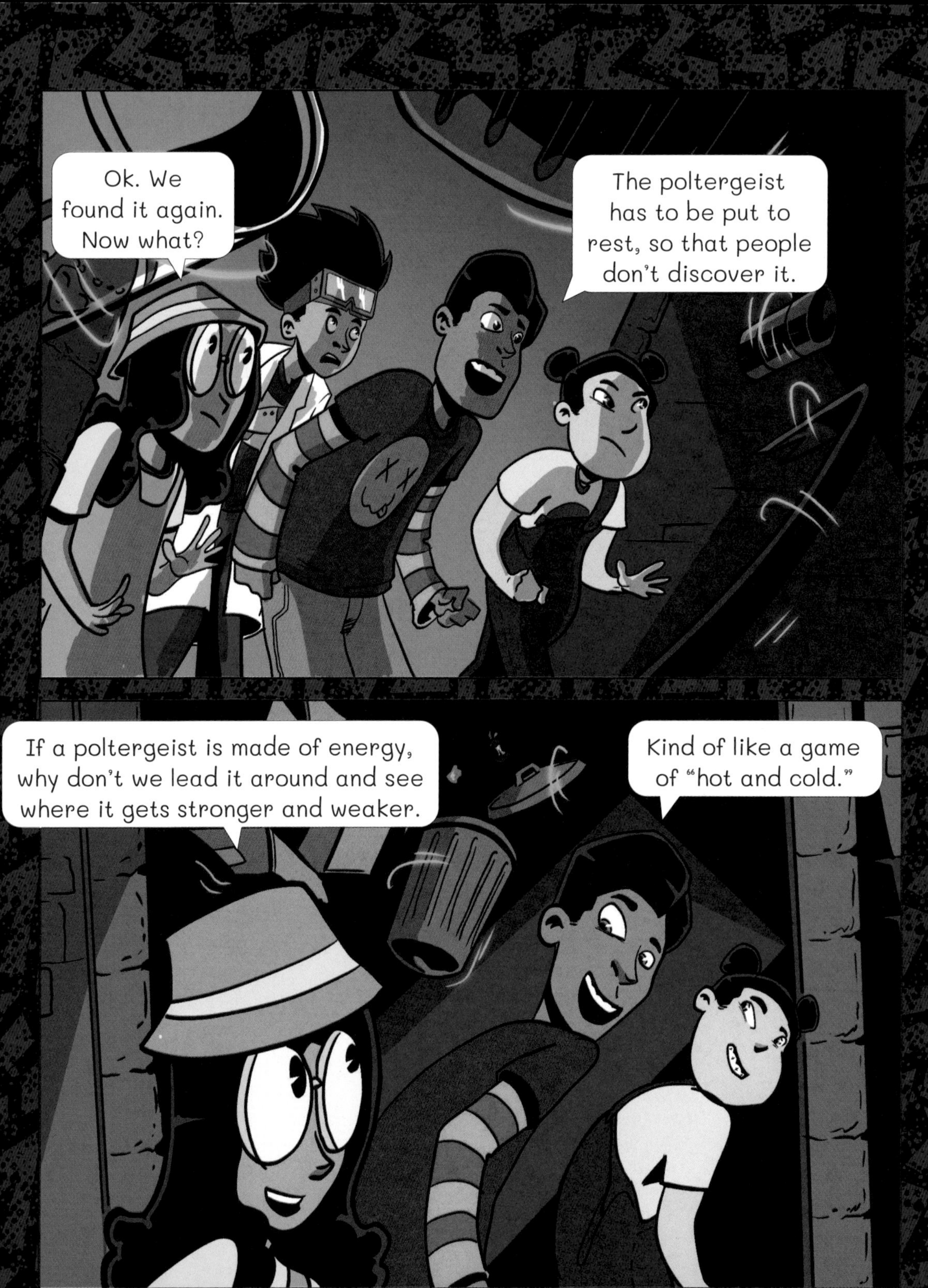
Ok. We found it again. Now what?
The poltergeist has to be put to rest, so that people don't discover it.
If a poltergeist is made of energy, why don't we lead it around and see where it gets stronger and weaker.
Kind of like a game of "hot and cold."

WHAT ARE POLTERGEISTS?

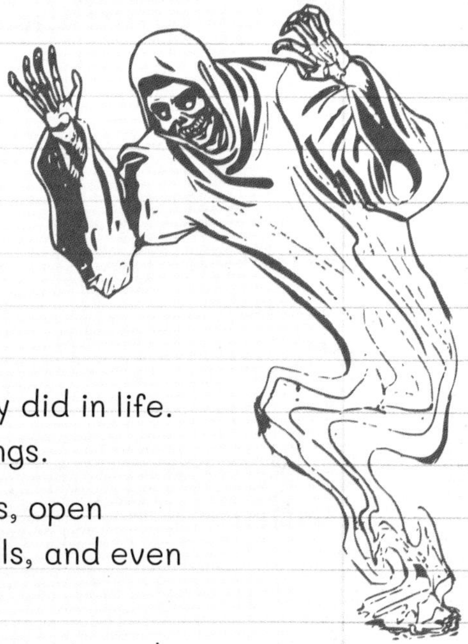

Poltergeists (from German, meaning "noisy ghost") are ghosts that can touch and move things. Like other ghosts, they are the spirits of dead people who repeat actions they did in life. But not all ghosts can move things.

* Poltergeists can move objects, open and close doors, knock on walls, and even make noises.
* They have sometimes been known to make objects appear and disappear.
* Some have even started fires.
* Poltergeists are known to **harass** and play games with humans.
* When poltergeist hauntings happen in a family's home, they are often associated with teenagers, especially girls.
* It is thought that the intensity of **adolescence** might attract poltergeists.
* Poltergeists aren't cruel, but their **mischief** can hurt people because they don't understand pain.

harass: to bother or scare continually

adolescence: the period of time when a child grows into an adult

mischief: misbehaving in a playful way

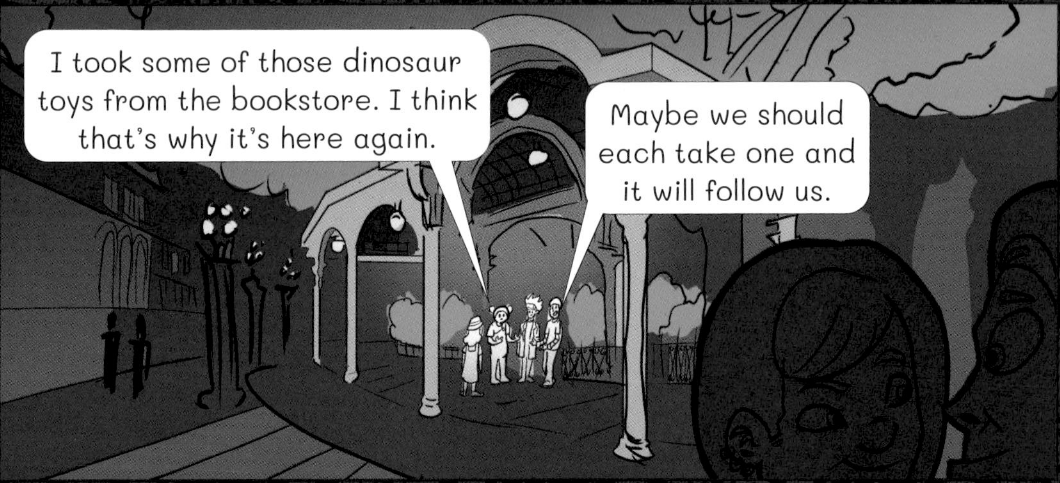
I took some of those dinosaur toys from the bookstore. I think that's why it's here again.
Maybe we should each take one and it will follow us.

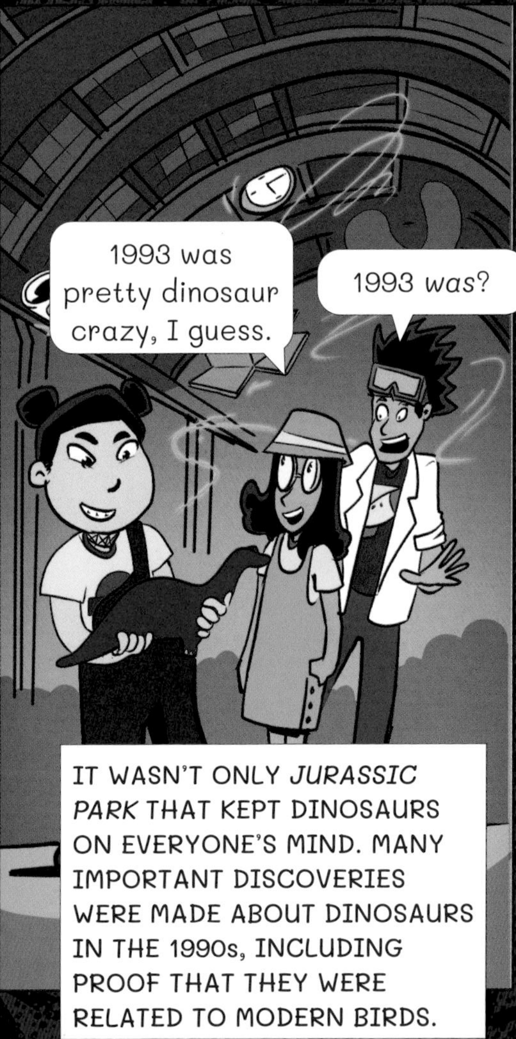
1993 was pretty dinosaur crazy, I guess.
1993 *was*?
IT WASN'T ONLY *JURASSIC PARK* THAT KEPT DINOSAURS ON EVERYONE'S MIND. MANY IMPORTANT DISCOVERIES WERE MADE ABOUT DINOSAURS IN THE 1990s, INCLUDING PROOF THAT THEY WERE RELATED TO MODERN BIRDS.

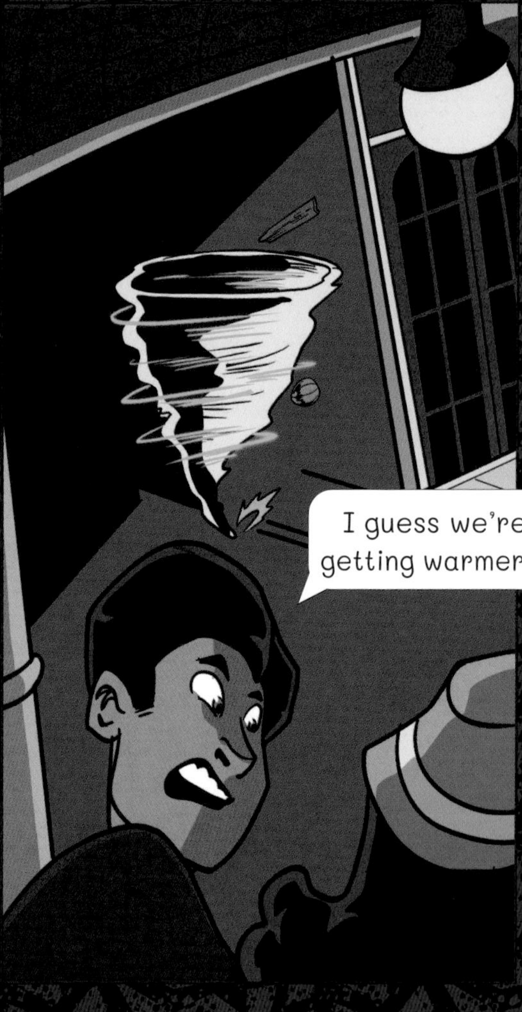
I guess we're getting warmer...

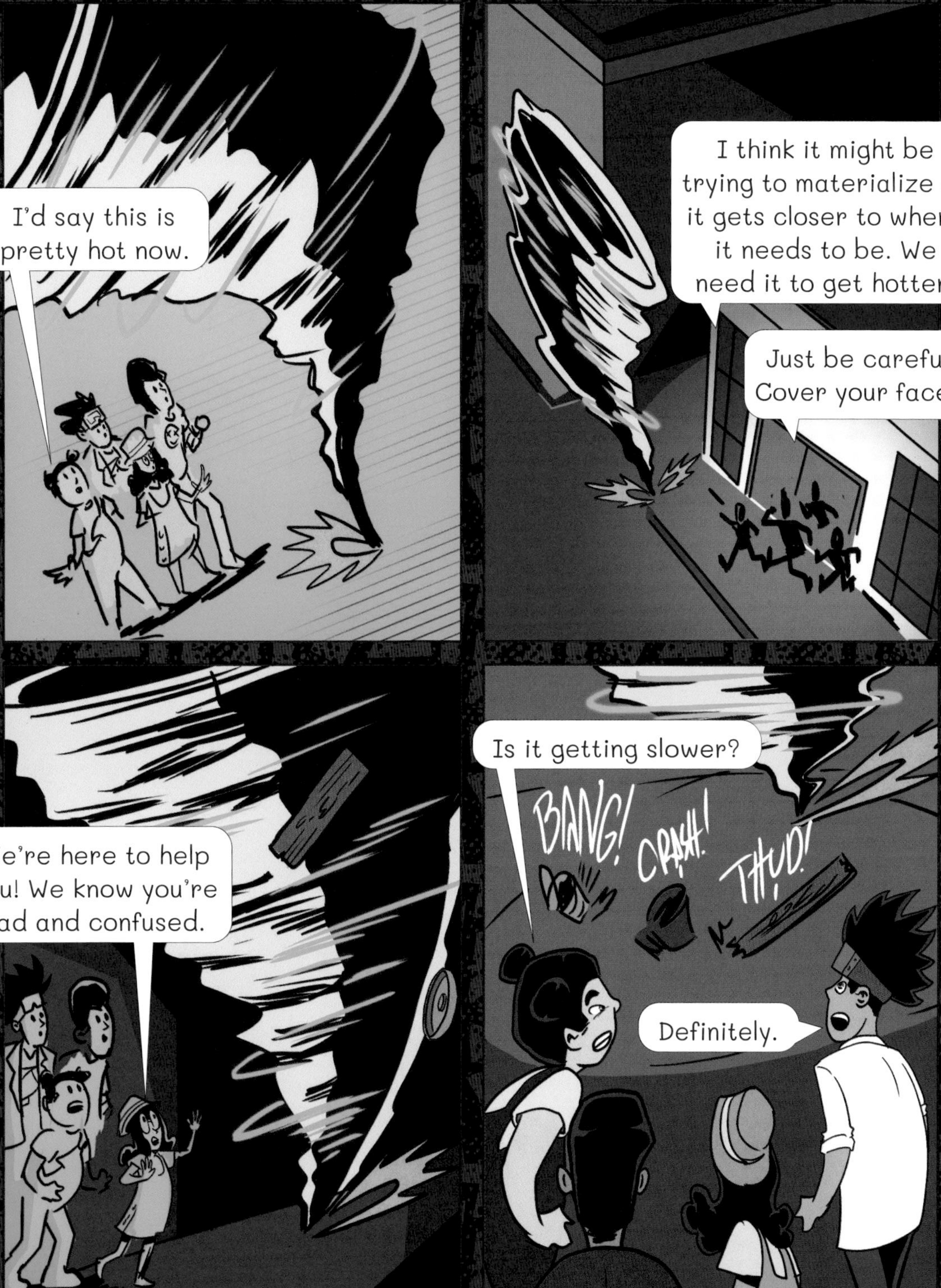
I'd say this is pretty hot now.
I think it might be trying to materialize as it gets closer to where it needs to be. We need it to get hotter.
Just be careful. Cover your faces.
We're here to help you! We know you're sad and confused.
Is it getting slower?
BANG!
CRASH!
THUD!
Definitely.

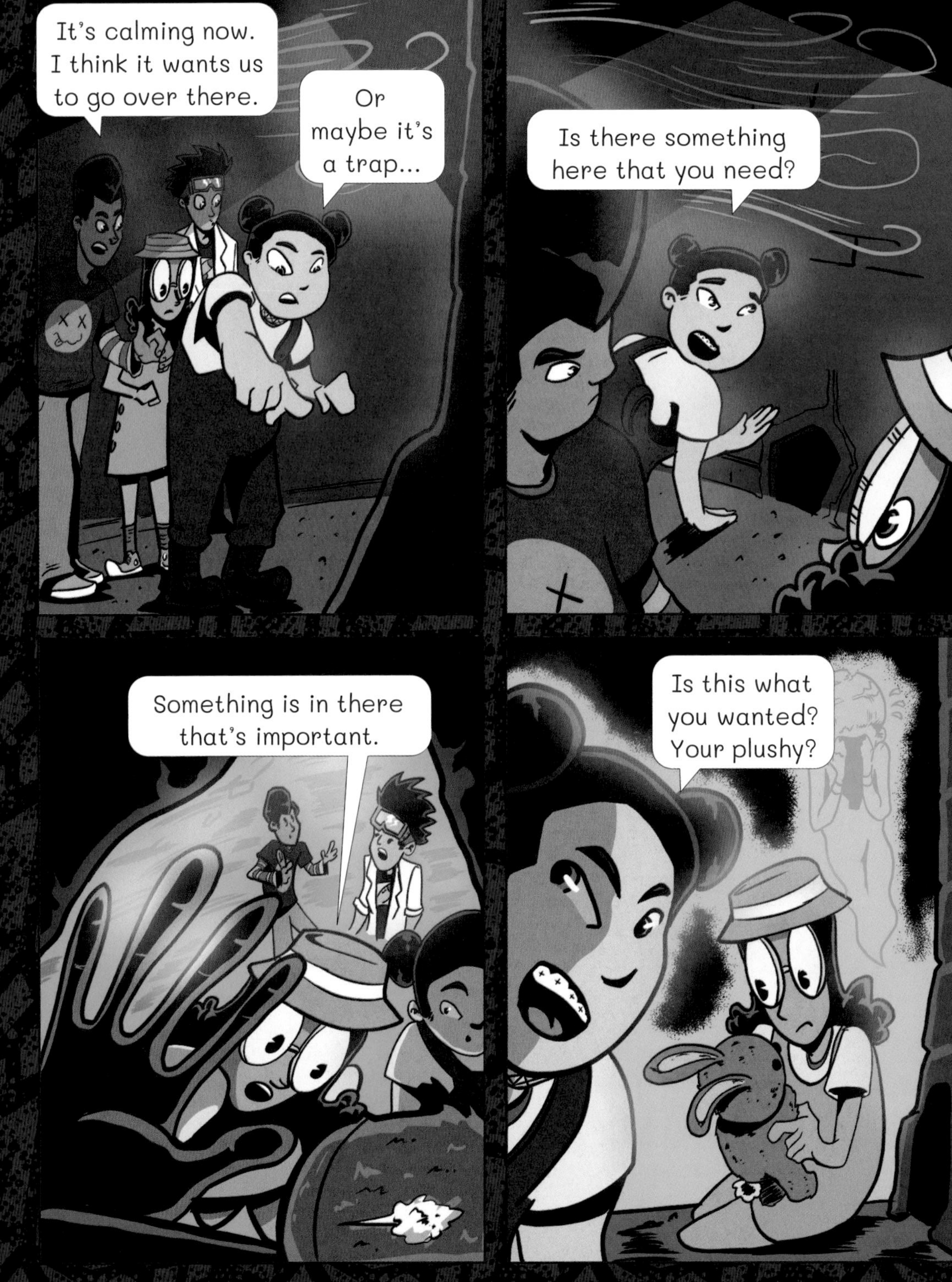
It's calming now. I think it wants us to go over there.
Or maybe it's a trap...
Is there something here that you need?
Something is in there that's important.
Is this what you wanted? Your plushy?

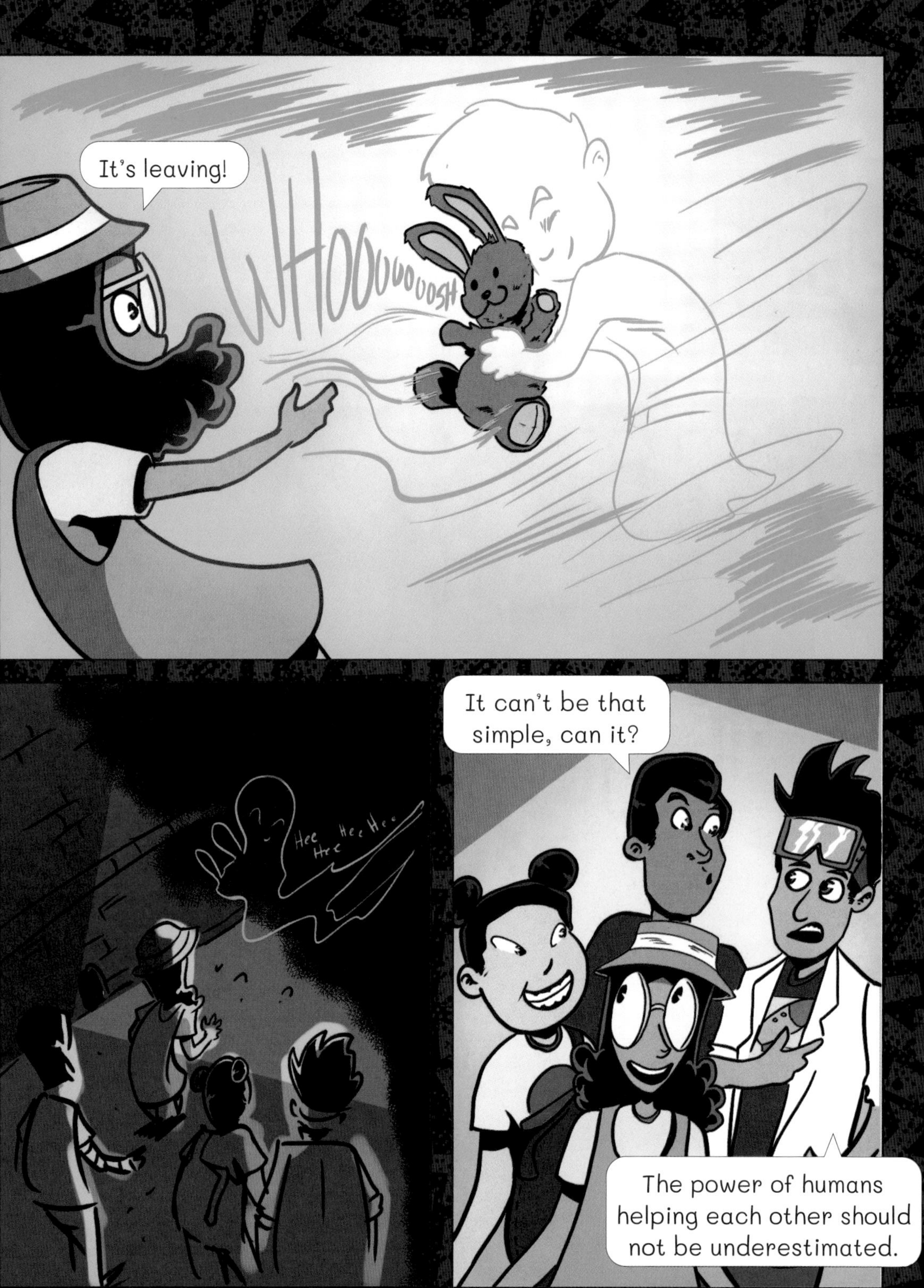
It's leaving!
WHOOOUUUUOOSH
It can't be that simple, can it?
Hee Hee Hee Hee
The power of humans helping each other should not be underestimated.

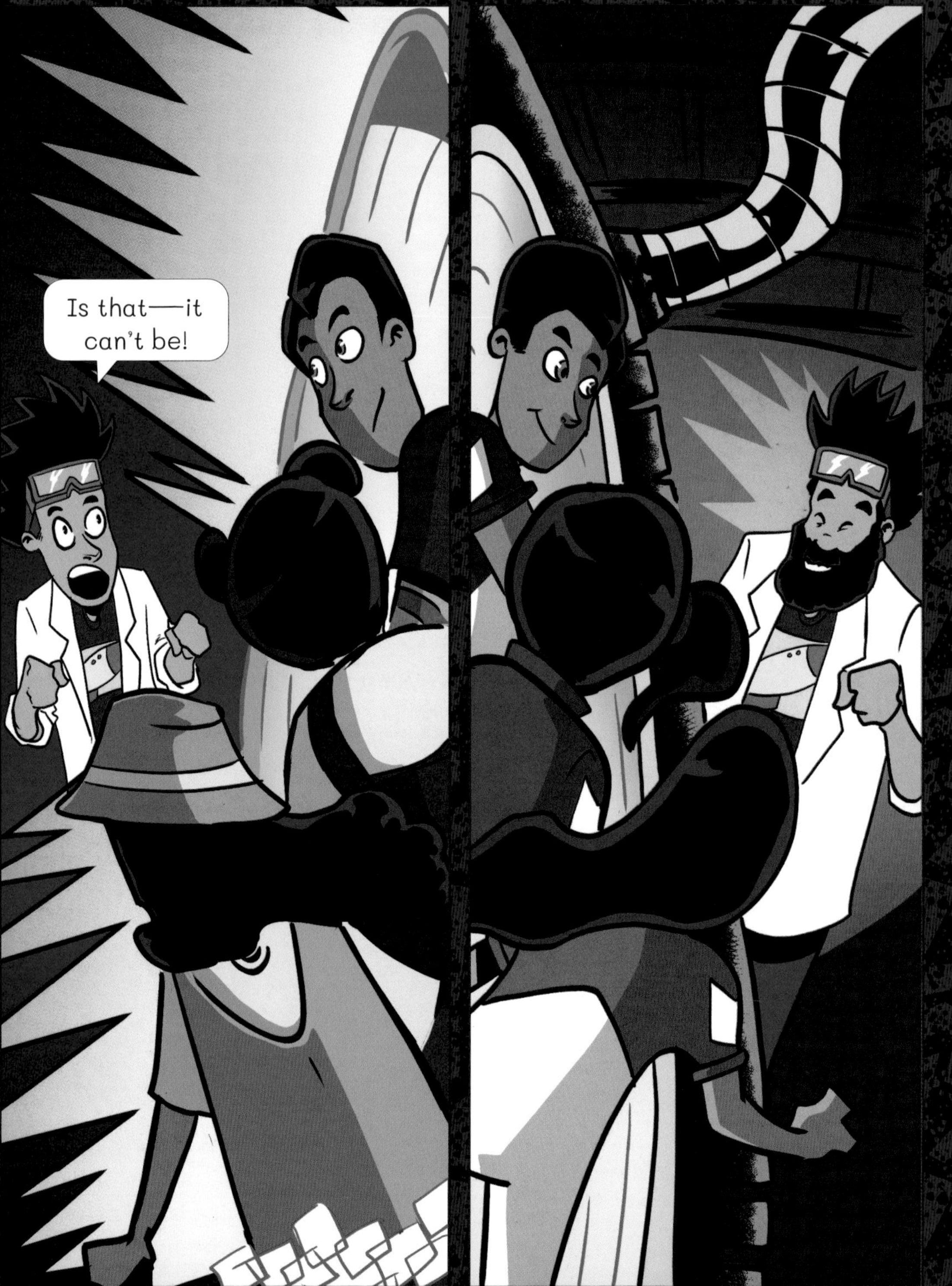
Is that—it can't be!

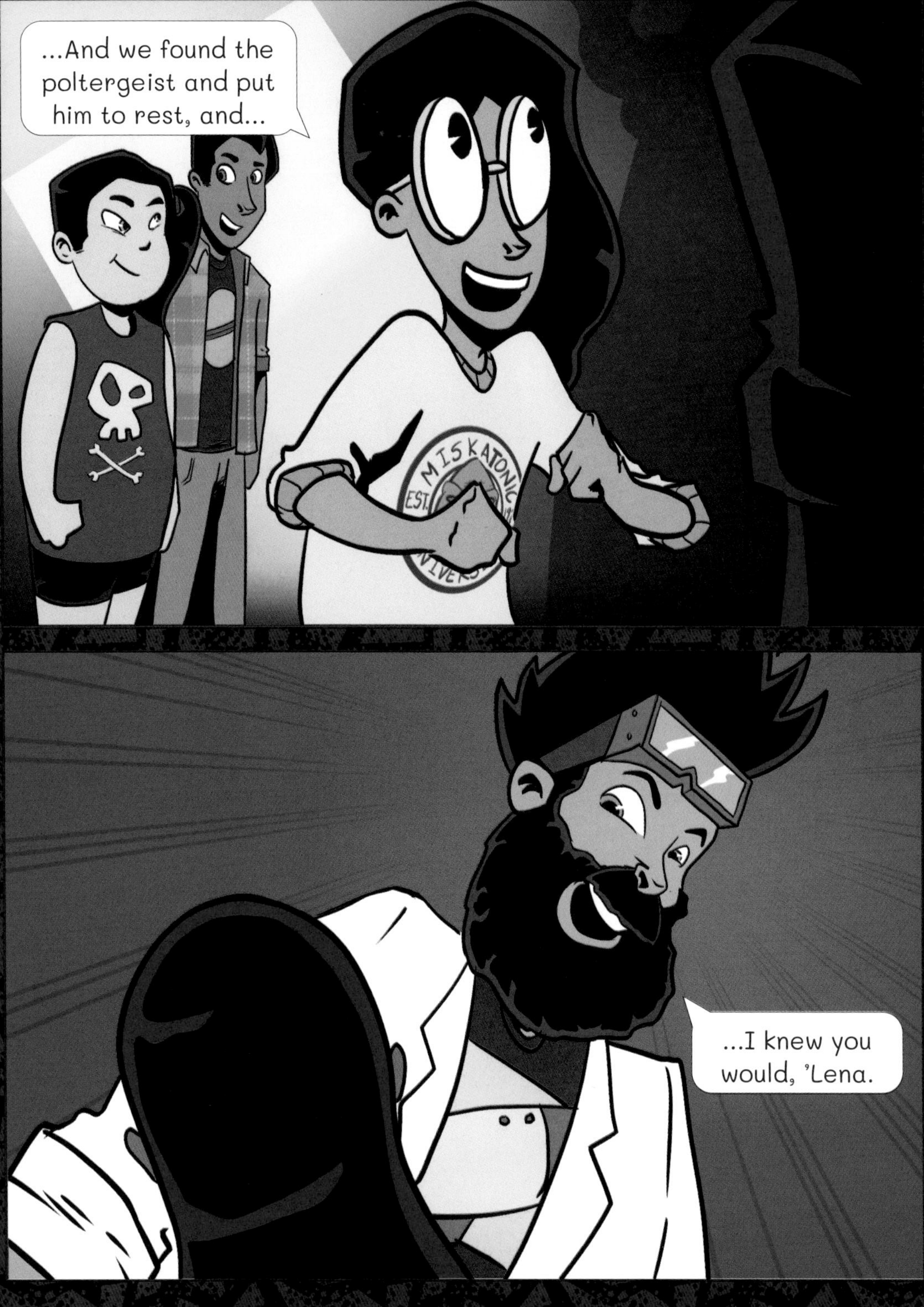
...And we found the poltergeist and put him to rest, and...
MISKATONIC
EST.
...I knew you would, 'Lena.

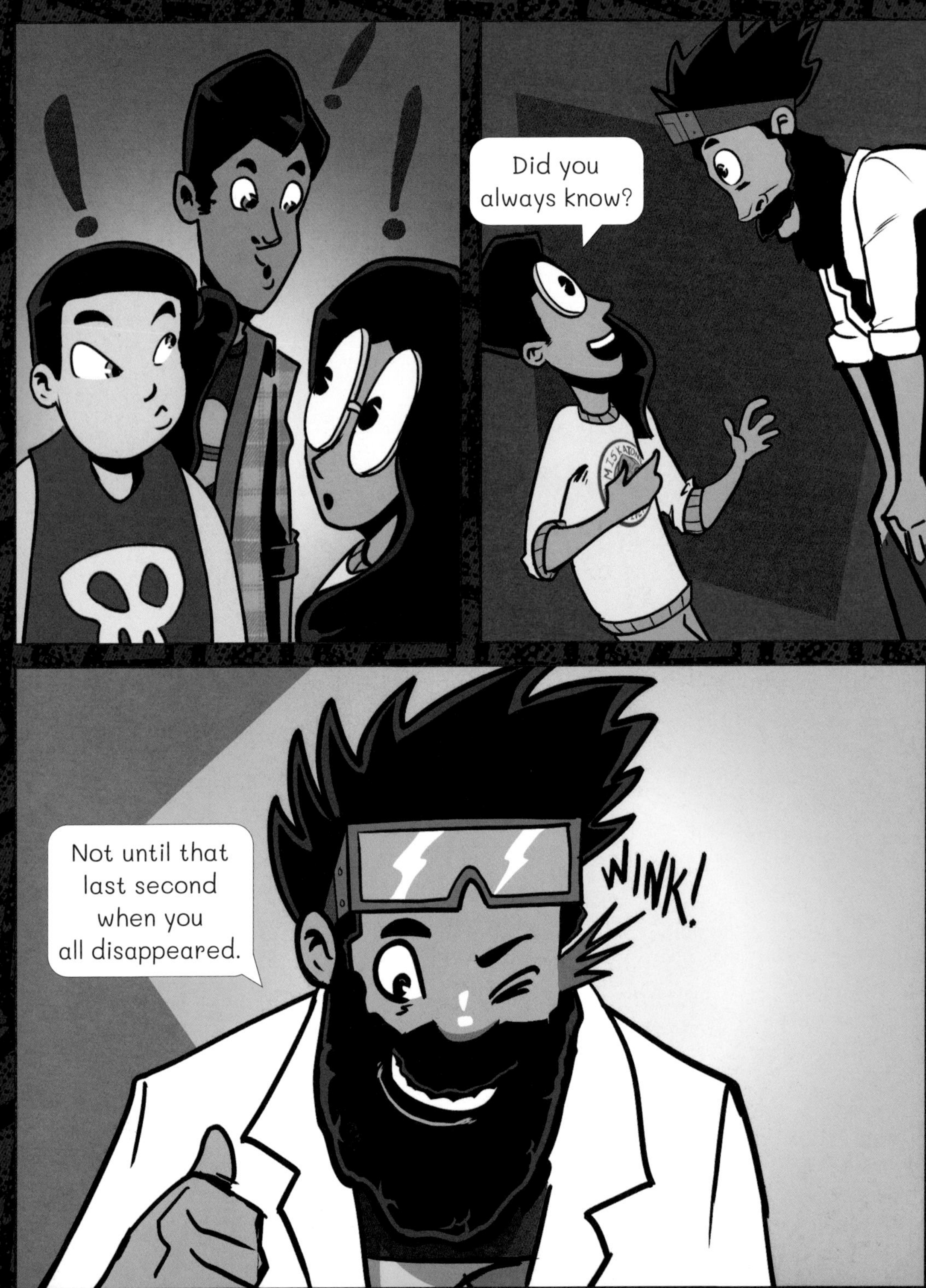
Did you always know?
Not until that last second when you all disappeared.
WINK!

SURVIVAL TIPS

Often, poltergeist activity increases slowly. It gets more intense before being resolved.

* When encountering a poltergeist, make sure your furniture is attached securely to the floor.

* You should shut breakable objects in cabinets.

* If the poltergeist keeps bothering you, make sure to tell an expert in the supernatural. They can help you rid yourself of the poltergeist.

* Humans can **bless** a poltergeist to help lay it to rest.

* A priest can do an **exorcism**.

* Because poltergeists are unhappy, bringing positive energy into the situation may help too.

bless: to say a special prayer for someone or something
exorcism: driving out evil spirits or ghosts

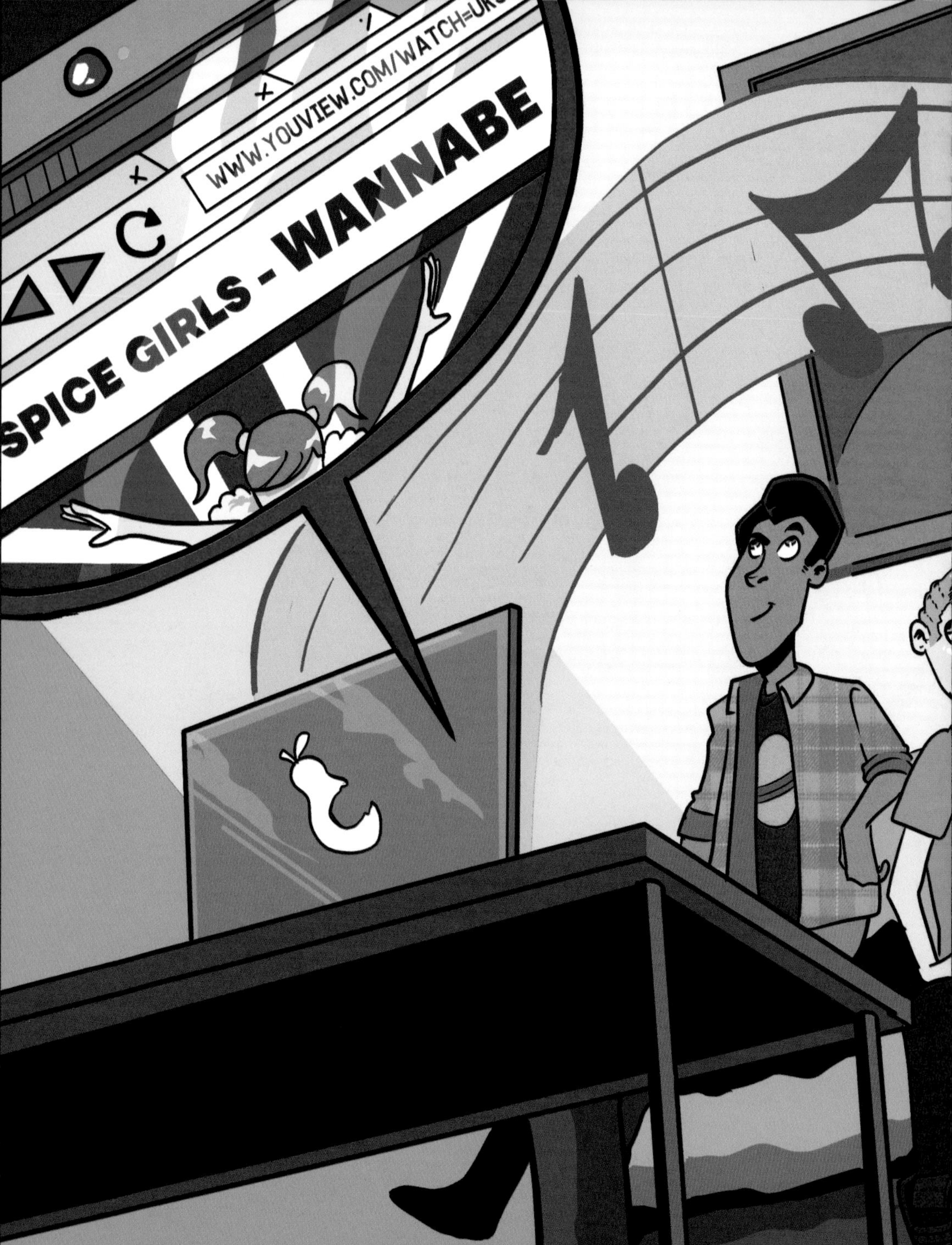
WWW.YOUVIEW.COM/WATCH=UR
SPICE GIRLS - WANNABE

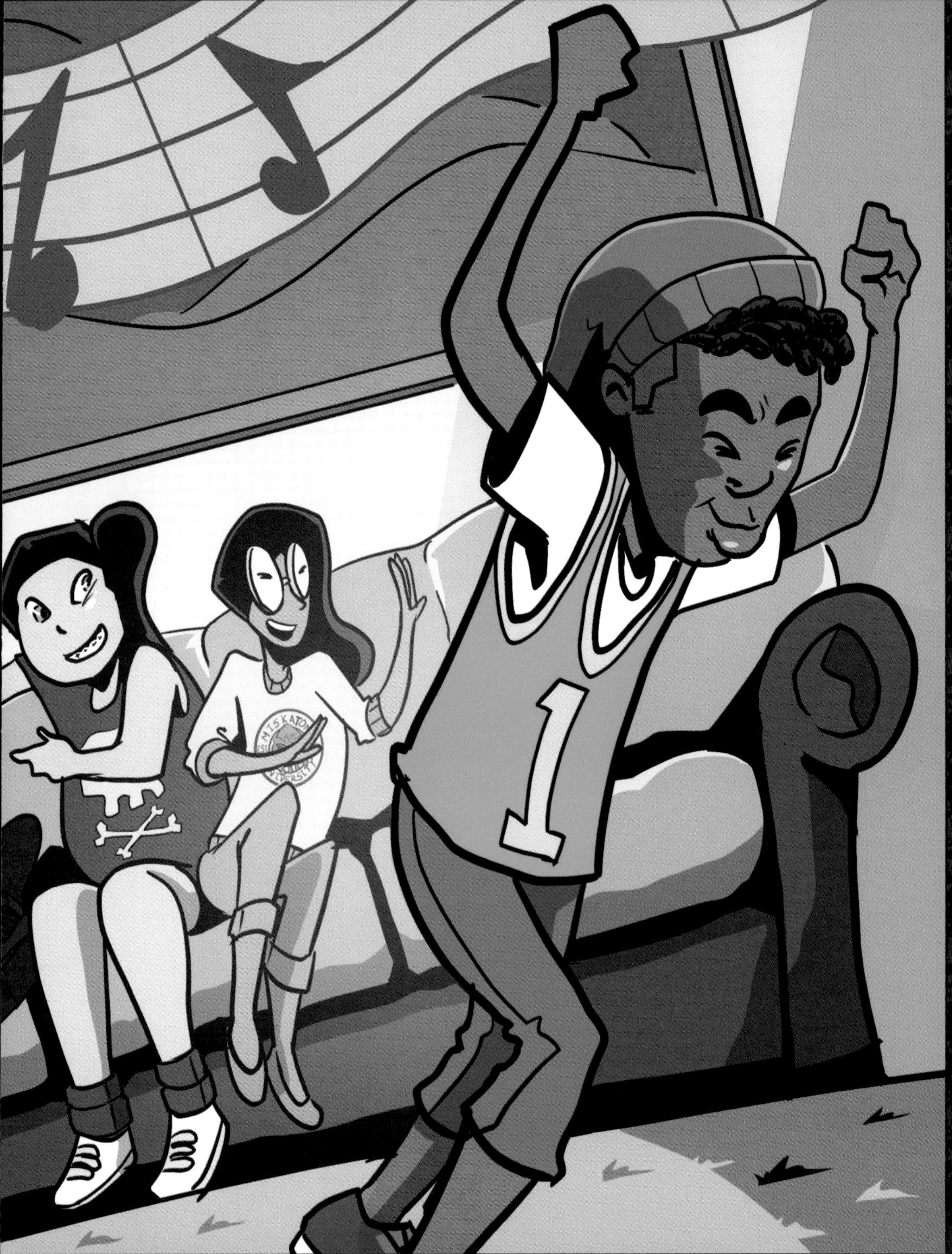

CREATE A 90s MUSIC MIX

Listening to music from the past can help inspire the music of the future. To better understand the 1990s, dive into the decade's music and make your own playlist!

Begin by looking up the top hits of the decade. Some artists you may find are:

* Mariah Carey
* Whitney Houston
* Alanis Morissette
* TLC
* Backstreet Boys

Other artists you may want to check out are mentioned in the text.

Using your favorite streaming service or YouTube, listen to as many different artists as you can. Choose 1 to 2 of your favorite songs to add to your own 90s playlist. Try to have at least 12 new songs.

Do any of these artists still record music today? How has their music changed?

Which song is your favorite from your playlist? Share it with friends and family. Which songs are their favorite?

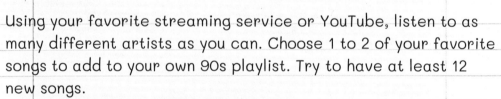

LEARN MORE

BOOKS

Weatherford, Carole Boston. *The Roots of Rap: 16 Bars on the 4 Pillars of Hip-Hop.* New York, NY: Little Bee Books, 2019.

Gregory, Josh. *Bill Clinton.* New York, NY: Children's Press, 2014.

Butler, Dori Hillestad. *The Underground Ghosts.* New York, NY: Grosset & Dunlap, 2017.

WEBSITES

Britannica—Seattle
https://www.britannica.com/place/Seattle-Washington

Ducksters—President Bill Clinton
https://www.ducksters.com/biography/uspresidents/billclinton.php

THE MONSTER HUNTER TEAM

JORGE
TÍO HECTOR'S NEPHEW, JORGE, LOVES MUSIC. AT 16 HE IS ONE OF THE OLDEST MONSTER HUNTERS AND THE LEADER OF THE GROUP.

MARCUS
MARCUS IS 14 AND IS WISE BEYOND HIS YEARS. HE IS A PROBLEM SOLVER, OFTEN GETTING THE GROUP OUT OF STICKY SITUATIONS.

FIONA
FIONA IS FIERCE AND PROTECTIVE. AT 16 SHE IS A ROLLER DERBY CHAMPION AND IS ONE OF JORGE'S CLOSEST FRIENDS.

ELENA
ELENA IS JORGE'S LITTLE SISTER AND TÍO HECTOR'S NIECE. AT 14, SHE IS THE HEART AND SOUL OF THE GROUP. ELENA IS KIND, THOUGHTFUL, AND SINCERE.

AMY
AMY IS 15. SHE LOVES BOOKS AND HISTORY. AMY AND ELENA SPEND ALMOST EVERY WEEKEND TOGETHER. THEY ARE ATTACHED AT THE HIP.

TÍO HECTOR
JORGE AND ELENA'S TIO IS THE MASTERMIND BEHIND THE MONSTER HUNTERS. HIS TIME TRAVEL MACHINE MAKES IT ALL POSSIBLE.

GLOSSARY

adolescence (ad-uh-LESS-ens) the period of time when a child grows into an adult

bless (BLES) to say a special prayer for someone or something

domestic terrorism (duh-MES-tik TEH-ror-ih-zum) terrorist acts where victims within the offender's own country are targeted

exorcism (EX-ur-sih-zum) driving out evil spirits or ghosts

harass (huh-RAS) to bother or scare continually

mischief (MISS-chif) misbehaving in a playful way

poltergeist (POL-tur-gaist) a ghost or supernatural being that causes loud noises, flying objects, and other physical disturbances

tío (TEE-oh) "uncle" in Spanish

INDEX